Going Places

Grand Canyon

Cari Meister

ABDO Publishing Company

visit us at
www.abdopub.com

Published by ABDO Publishing Company 4940 Viking Drive, Edina, Minnesota 55435.
Copyright © 2000 by Abdo Consulting Group, Inc. International copyrights reserved in all
countries. No part of this book may be reproduced in any form without written permission
from the publisher.

Printed in the United States.

Photo credits: Peter Arnold, Inc.

Edited by Lori Kinstad Pupeza
Contributing editor Morgan Hughes
Graphics by Linda O'Leary

Library of Congress Cataloging-in-Publication Data

Meister, Cari.
  Grand Canyon / Cari Meister.
    p. cm. -- (Going Places)
  Includes index.
  Summary: Describes the history, geographic features, and plant and animal life of
  the natural wonder known as the Grand Canyon and the activities of visitors to
  Grand Canyon National Park.
  ISBN 1-57765-024-7
  1. Grand Canyon (Ariz.)--Juvenile literature. [1. Grand Canyon (Ariz.) 2.
  Grand Canyon National Park (Ariz.) 3. National parks and reserves.] I. Title.
  II. Series: Meister, Cari. Going places.
  F788.M44 2000
  917.91'320453--dc21   98-4809
                                                                          CIP
                                                                          AC

Contents

The Largest Canyon

*T*he Grand Canyon is the largest canyon in the world. It is 277 miles (446 km) long, as much as 18 miles (29 km) wide, and covers over a million acres (439,076 hectares) of land. That's about 800,000 football fields!

People visit Grand Canyon National Park from all over the world. More than five million **tourists** visit the park in northern Arizona each year.

People visit the Grand Canyon for different reasons. Most people come to see the canyon's beauty and wonder. Some people come to study the canyon's rocks and wildlife.

People can enjoy the canyon in different ways. Some people choose to view the canyon by helicopters or airplanes. Other people want to hike and camp. Some people ride mules to the

The south rim of the Grand Canyon.

bottom of the canyon. Brave people test their skills **white-water** rafting down the Colorado River. The Colorado River runs through the canyon on its way from Colorado to Mexico.

There are many things to do at Grand Canyon National Park. How will you ever choose?

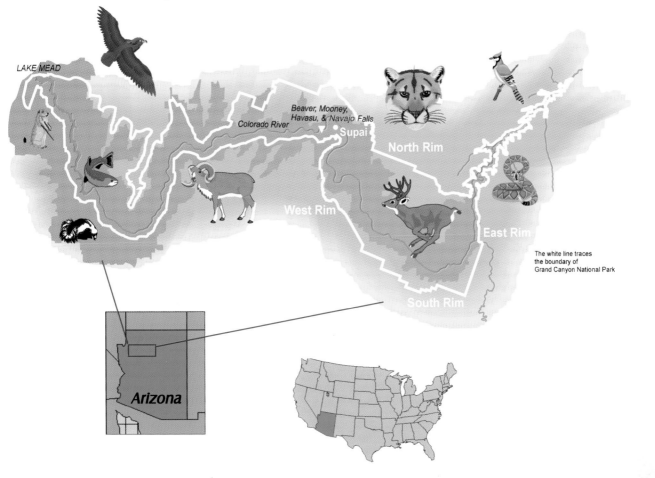

LAKE MEAD

Colorado River

Beaver, Mooney, Havasu, & Navajo Falls

Supai

North Rim

West Rim

East Rim

South Rim

The white line traces the boundary of Grand Canyon National Park

Arizona

The Layers Tell a Story

*B*efore you jump into a raft, or ride on top of a mule, you should know a little about the canyon.

The Grand Canyon is made up of many layers. Sandstone, limestone, shale, and other rocks make up the layers. The different layers tell us a story. They tell us that some of the rocks in the canyon are two billion years old. That's even before the time when dinosaurs lived!

The layers also tell us that the canyon is always changing. At one time the Grand Canyon was covered in sand. At another time the Grand Canyon was a mountain range, higher than the Rocky Mountains.

About six million years ago the Colorado River started to cut away at the layers. The river was much bigger and more powerful than it is today. The powerful **erosion** caused by the river formed the Grand Canyon. Today, the Colorado River continues to make changes in the canyon.

The Colorado River has been eroding away the Grand Canyon for millions of years.

The Havasupai

*M*any people have made the Grand Canyon their home. **Native Americans** have lived in or around the canyon for over 4,000 years.

Today, about 650 members of the Havasupai tribe live in the village of Supai. Havasupai means "people of the green-blue water." Their name comes from the color of water that flows near their home.

There are four waterfalls on the Havasupai **reservation**. Havasu Falls, Mooney Falls, Navajo Falls, and Beaver Falls bring many **tourists** to the reservation.

The village of Supai is located at the bottom of the canyon. To get to Supai from the canyon's rim, there is an eight mile (13 km) trail. You can only reach Supai by foot or by riding a horse.

The Havasupai show tourists around the canyon. They also farm, ride in rodeos, and **preserve** the land. The Havasupai believe that preserving the land is a sacred duty. By preserving the land they are preserving their way of life.

The blue-green colored water that runs through the Grand Canyon gave the Havasupai their name.

John Wesley Powell

*I*f you look at a map from the early 1860s, you will not see the Grand Canyon. It was there, but it hadn't been **explored** yet by white **settlers**. Many people were too scared of the Colorado River's raging waters to travel through the canyon.

Then, in 1869, a one-armed man climbed aboard a boat. His name was John Wesley Powell. John was a man of great skill and courage. Dangerous waters did not scare him. John had seen danger before. He lost his arm fighting in the Civil War.

John and his crew set out to explore the Grand Canyon. They wanted to **navigate** the Colorado River. It was a difficult and dangerous job. The men faced rough waters, storms, and extreme temperatures.

There were times when they had little to eat. Despite all of the hardships, they succeeded. In 1869, the Grand Canyon was mapped.

John Wesley Powell (R), shown here with Paiute Chief Tau-Gu, explored the Grand Canyon before it was mapped.

Canyon Wildlife

*T*he Grand Canyon is home to a wide variety of animals. Many different kinds of animals can live here because there are many different **climates**. Mountain lions, rainbow trout, bighorn sheep, and the red-spotted toad can all be found in the Grand Canyon.

The forests of the north rim can get cold and wet. Look closely. In the forests, you may spot a white-tailed kaibab squirrel or an elk. The inner canyon is hot and dry. Watch your feet! Scorpions and rattlesnakes live here.

Over 300 species of birds live in the Grand Canyon. There are more peregrine falcons in the Grand Canyon than anywhere else in the **continental United States**.

The humpback chub lives in the Colorado River. This strange looking fish has a hump and a narrow tail. The humpback chub is one of many animals in the Grand Canyon in danger of becoming **extinct**. The **Endangered Species Act** helps protect these animals.

Mountain lions live in the Grand Canyon.

Canyon Plants

*D*id you know that prickly pear is not a fruit? Prickly pear is a cactus. But, the fruit from the prickly pear plant makes great syrup, jelly, and candy. It is a desert dessert.

Prickly pear is one of the many types of **cacti** that grow in the Grand Canyon. Some cacti, like the prickly pear, grow yellow flowers. Other cacti grow pink or red flowers.

The buckhorn cholla grows yellow flowers. Some **Native American** tribes steamed buckhorn cholla flower buds for food. They took the buds from the plant very carefully. If they moved quickly they risked being poked. Cacti often have sharp spikes or bristles for protection.

Cacti are not the only type of **vegetation** in the Grand Canyon. Ponderosa pine trees hug the rim. Aspen, fir, and spruce trees grow on the highest parts of the canyon's rim. You may spot juniper and piñon trees if you visit the south side of the canyon.

This prickly pear cactus grows in the Grand Canyon.

White-water Adventure

*P*ut on your life jacket. Gather your courage. Get ready for the ride of your life!

Many **tourists** visit the Grand Canyon to raft down the Colorado River. Rafters meet their guide at Lee's Ferry. The guide explains that rafting is dangerous. The river is very strong. People sometimes get thrown from the raft.

The guide tells about major rapids and **white water**. After hearing about the danger, some people leave. Other people climb aboard. The guide gets in the raft, too. He carries two sets of oars. One set is for calm water. The other set is for rough water.

At first the river seems as smooth as glass. The wind picks up. Little splashes. Big splashes. Soon the water is raging. The waves roar. The guide moves the raft through the water. All of a sudden, the water is calm. The rafters catch their breath and wait for the next rapid.

White-water rapids.

Riding a Mule

One way to see the Grand Canyon is by mule. There are one day mule trips. For those people who love animals and the outdoors, there are two day mule trips.

Mule trips start up on the rims. Here, riders meet their guides. They also meet the mules that will take them deep into the canyon.

Mules are stubborn animals. Sometimes they don't want to move. Even the guides have trouble with them. Even though mules are stubborn, they travel well in the canyon. Mules are sturdy animals.

The first part of the journey is downhill. Mules step carefully down the trail. As the mules get lower and lower, the weather may change. Before starting on a mule ride, it is important to find out what clothes to bring.

On mule trips, half of the time is spent climbing down. Half of the time is spent climbing up. On two day mule trips, riders sleep at Phantom Ranch.

Tourists hike and ride horses and mules on trails through the Grand Canyon.

A National Treasure

*T*here are many things to do at Grand Canyon National Park. You do not have to go **white-water** rafting or ride a mule to **explore** the Grand Canyon's beauty. There are many hiking trails and lookout points.

Hiking trails and lookout points are spread throughout the park. The three main trails are the Bright Angel, the South Kaibab, and the North Kaibab.

The Grand Canyon Theater at Tusayan shows films on a screen six stories high. Here you can see what it is like to go white-water rafting without ever getting wet. You can also see what it is like to ride a mule without getting a sore back end.

The Grand Canyon is an amazing work of nature. The beauty and splendor of the Grand Canyon cannot be seen anywhere else in the world.

Visit and see what you think.

The Grand Canyon is an amazing work of nature.

Glossary

Cacti: the plural of cactus; more than one cactus plant.

Climate: the weather conditions in a certain area.

Continental United States: the 48 mainland states; all states but Alaska and Hawaii.

Endangered Species Act: laws that protect animals that are in danger of becoming extinct.

Erosion: the process of wearing away.

Explored: to look into or travel over and examine carefully.

Extinct: no longer existing or alive.

Navigate: to sail through a body of water.

Native American: American Indians. People whose ancestors originated in the Americas.

Preserve: to keep safe and undisturbed.

Reservation: land set aside for Native Americans.

Settlers: a group of people who establish homes in a new territory.

Tourists: people who travel to visit a place for fun.

Vegetation: plants.

White water: extremely rough areas of water.

Internet Sites

Canadian CultureNet
http://www.culturenet.ucalgary.ca/
CultureNet is a World Wide Web window on Canadian culture. It is a home for Canadian cultural networks.

The Disney World Explorer
http://www.disney.com/DisneyInteractive/WDWExplorer/
This is a fun and colorful site with trivia games, maps, previews, downloads, CD-ROM helpers and much, much more.

Grand Canyon Association
http://www.thecanyon.com/gca/
You're just a click away from a backpacking trip, a chance to meet canyon lovers like you, and books on this great region. This site has some great artwork.

Mexconnect
http://www.mexconnect.com/
This site has great travel ideas, Mexican art, tradition, food, history, and much more. It includes a chat room, tour section, and photo gallery.

Fantastic Journeys Yellowstone
http://www.nationalgeographic.com/features/97/yellowstone/index.html
Explore Yellowstone National Park, a place like no other on Earth. See strange marvels, go underground to find what causes them, and trigger an eruption of the famous geyser Old Faithful. A very cool site!

Marine Watch
http://www.marinewatch.com/
Welcome to Marine Watch, the international news journal about events occurring on, under and over the oceans of the planet. This site has many links and cool photos!

These sites are subject to change.

Pass It On

Adventure Enthusiasts: Tell us about places you've been or want to see. A national park, amusement park, or any exciting place you want to tell us about. We want to hear from you!

To get posted on the ABDO Publishing Company website E-mail us at
"Adventure@abdopub.com"
Visit the ABDO Publishing Company website at www.abdopub.com

Index